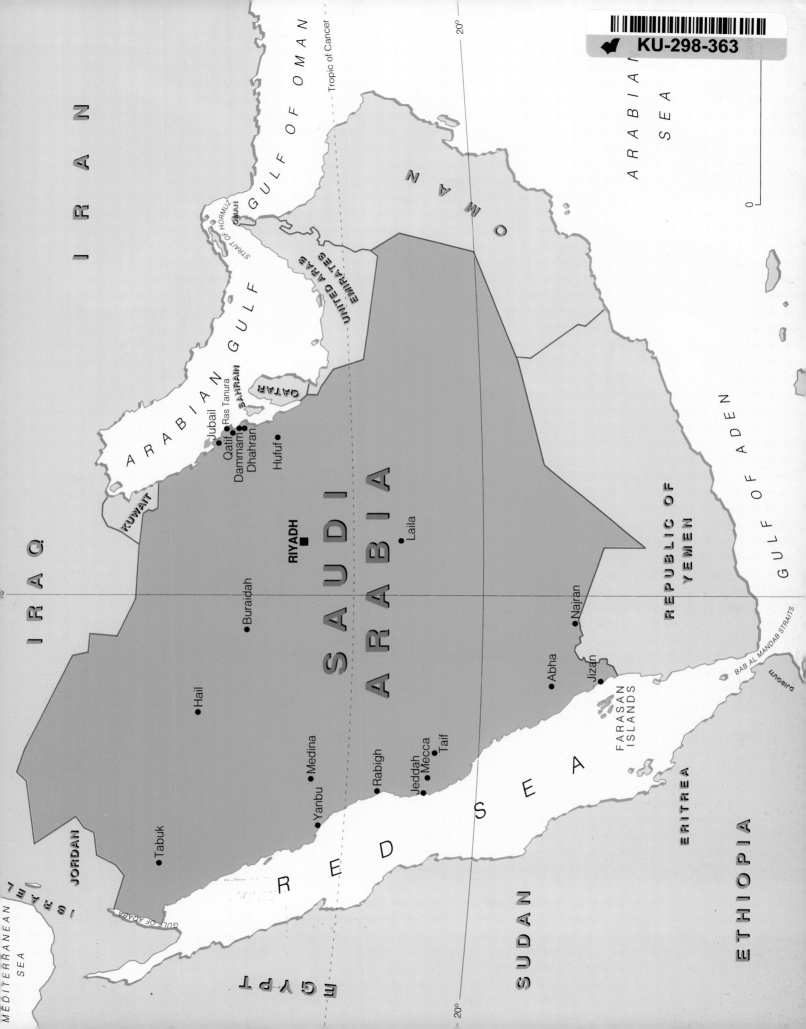

COUNTRY
FACT
FILES

Saudi Arabia

Susannah Honeyman

SIMON & SCHUSTER
YOUNG BOOKS

First published in 1994 by Simon & Schuster Young Books
© Simon & Schuster Young Books 1994

Simon & Schuster Young Books
Campus 400
Maylands Avenue
Hemel Hempstead
Herts HP2 7EZ

Design Roger Kohn
Editor Diana Russell
DTP editor Helen Swansbourne
Picture research Valerie Mulcahy
Illustration János Márffy
Consultant Don Kerr
Commissioning editor Debbie Fox

We are grateful to the following for permission
to reproduce photographs:
Front Cover: TRIP/Helene Rogers *above*, R Warburton/Middle
East Pictures *below;* Aspect Picture Library, pages 24 *above*
(Don Smetzer), 25 and 35 *above* (Peter Carmichael);
Associated Press/Topham Picture Source, page 17 *left*; J Allan
Cash Photolibrary, page 14 *below*; Robert Harding Picture
Library, pages 8 *below* (Peter Ryan), 11, 13 (James Green), 18
(David Lomax), 30 (James Green), 39 *below*; Magnum, pages
19 *above* (Abbas), 26 *below* (Bruno Barbey), 40 (Abbas); The
Military Picture Library, page 28 (Geoff Lee); Christine
Osborne/Middle East Pictures, pages 10, 31 *above*; Oxford
Scientific Films, page 38 (Eyal Bartov); Picturepoint, pages 16
(Tomkinson), 23, 24, *below*, 33 *above*; Peter Sanders
Photography, pages 12/13, 14/15, 22 *above*, 31 *below*, 34
below; Frank Spooner Pictures/Gamma, pages 8 *above*, 20
and 26 *above* (Halstead), 27 (D E Keerle), 42 (Laurent van der
Stockt); Tony Stone Images, pages 9, 32; Sygma, page 37 (J
Langevin); TRIP/Helene Rogers, pages 12, 17 *right*, 19 *below*,
21, 22 *below*, 29, 33 *below*, 34 *above*, 35 *below*, 36, 39 *above;*
R Warburton/Middle East Pictures, page 41

Grateful thanks to the Meteorological Office, Bracknell, for
supplying information for the chart on page 15

The statistics given in this book are the most up to date
available at the time of going to press

Printed and bound in Hong Kong by Paramount Printing Group

A CIP catalogue record for this book is available from
the British Library

ISBN: 0 7500 1486 5

CONTENTS

Words that are explained in the glossary are printed in
SMALL CAPITALS the first time they are mentioned in the text.

INTRODUCTION

The kingdom of Saudi Arabia was created more than 60 years ago, in 1932. The people of this ancient homeland of the Arabs were mainly poor farmers and NOMADIC herders, who struggled to make a living among the hottest deserts on Earth. Some merchants in the towns traded with East Africa, Persia (Iran) and India in small wooden ships, just as their ancestors had done in the Middle Ages.

Today Saudi Arabia is one of the richest and most powerful states in the world.

In the 1930s American prospectors discovered oil in the country. Today Saudi Arabia has the biggest oil reserves and is the biggest exporter of oil in the world. Since the 1960s it has earned billions of dollars from its oil, and has used its wealth to build modern cities and services, and strong armed forces too.

But Saudi Arabia is also powerful for another reason. Islam was founded there in the 7th century AD, and soon spread through northern Africa, the Middle East and the Far East. Now one-seventh of the world's population is Moslem, and Saudi Arabia is their holy land. Every day 2,000

▲ *All over the world people depend on Saudi oil and gas for needs like petrol and kerosene, electricity, plastics, medicines, fertilizer and synthetic fibres.*

million people in more than 70 countries face in the direction of Mecca, in Saudi Arabia, to pray. And every year up to 2 million Moslems travel to Saudi Arabia on PILGRIMAGE to the most sacred places of Islam.

Wealth has changed the life-style of most Saudi people, through education, health-care, modern housing and transport. But everyday life in Saudi Arabia is still based on religious beliefs and customs that are stricter than in almost any other Moslem country, except Iran. Traditional ways and advanced technology exist side by side.

▶ *These ancient rock tombs were built by the Nabateans of north-west Arabia. For 400 years, up to AD 105, the Nabateans controlled overland trade from Yemen, India and Persia (Iran) to the Roman Empire.*

SAUDI ARABIA AT A GLANCE

- Area: 2,150,000 square kilometres
- Population (1992 estimate): 12,304,835 Saudi nationals, plus 4,624,459 foreign workers (total 16,929,294)
- Population density: 6.5 people per square kilometre
- Capital: Riyadh, population 1.7 million
- Other main cities: Jeddah 1 million; Mecca 460,000; Medina 320,000; Taif 250,000; Dammam–Dhahran 250,000
- Highest mountain: Mount Sawdah, 3,207 metres
- Language: Arabic
- Religion: Islam (98% Sunni Moslems; 2% Shia Moslems)
- Literacy (1987): 52%
- Currency: Saudi riyal, written as SR, divided into 100 halalah (5 halalah = 1 piastre)
- Economy: Based on oil and gas production and exports, with developing industry, agriculture and banking
- Major resources: Oil and gas reserves
- Major products: Crude and refined oil and gas products
- Environmental problems: Shortage of water, advancing desert, oil pollution

▶ *Mecca, the birthplace of the Prophet Mohammed, contains the most sacred place in Islam: the Ka'aba shrine. It is at the centre of the Great* MOSQUE, *draped in black cloth decorated with verses from the* KORAN *woven in gold. Every Moslem has a religious duty to try to make a pilgrimage to Mecca.*

LANDSCAPE

Saudi Arabia is a land of deserts, of many kinds. There are rugged mountain ranges, "seas" of sand, rocky plains, salt flats and plateaus with deep gorges and dry valleys. It is one of the most hostile environments on Earth for people, but it is also a land of variety, with areas of great natural beauty.

The country occupies 80% of the Arabian PENINSULA, which began to break away from the continent of Africa 35 million years ago. As they parted, the ocean flooded the northern Great Rift Valley to form the Red Sea.

The wedge-shaped peninsula is bounded on the west by the Red Sea and on the east by the Arabian Gulf and Arabian Sea. In the north, desert forms a natural barrier between Saudi Arabia and neighbouring Jordan, Iraq and Kuwait. There are land borders in the east with the United Arab Emirates and Qatar, while the tiny island state of Bahrain lies off the coast. In the south-east, mountains separate Saudi Arabia from Oman and Yemen.

The Hejaz Mountains run parallel to the Red Sea for 1,600 kilometres, from Medina to the Gulf of Aqaba. In the southern Hejaz the ranges reach 3,000 metres and average 1,500 metres at the northern end. Raised fossil coral reefs form sheer cliffs, broken by narrow inlets. Exposed coral reefs in the southern Red Sea form the Farasan Islands.

Until 600 years ago, there were active

▲ *The shallow waters of the Arabian Gulf meet the low-lying desert plain of Eastern Province in a network of tidal creeks.*

KEY FACTS

● Arabia is moving away from Africa at the rate of 4 centimetres a year.
● The average depth of the Arabian Gulf is only 35 metres and its deepest point is 100 metres. The Red Sea reaches 2,850 metres in depth.
● Al-Rub' al-Khali is the largest sand desert in the world – bigger than France, Belgium and the Netherlands combined.
● Traditional houses in Jeddah are built from ancient coral rock cut from the Red Sea coast.
● Some villages in remote valleys in the Asir can only be reached by using rope ladders.

◄ *Al-Rub' al-Khali. Ridges and dunes of red sand formed by fierce monsoon rains during the last Ice Age tower 300 metres above white salt flats.*

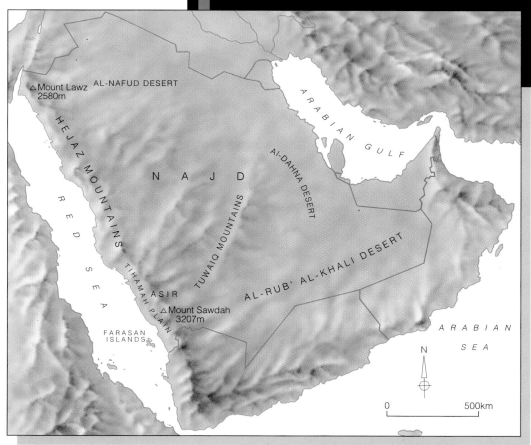

AL-NAFUD DESERT

△ Mount Lawz 2580m

HEJAZ MOUNTAINS

RED SEA

N A J D

AL-DAHNA DESERT

ARABIAN GULF

TUWAIQ MOUNTAINS

AL-RUB' AL-KHALI DESERT

ASIR

TIHAMAH PLAIN

△ Mount Sawdah 3207m

FARASAN ISLANDS

ARABIAN SEA

N

0   500km

Asir Province in the south-west has the country's highest mountains and, on the Red Sea coast, old lava flows and mangrove swamps. TERRACES *on the slopes make full use of the soil and climate here, which are suited to arable farming.*

volcanoes in western Saudi Arabia. But all that remains today are black boulders of volcanic rock called basalt, scattered over the plains and mountain slopes.

The remote south-western Asir region is also mountainous, averaging 1,500 metres but with higher peaks, including the highest in the country, Mount Sawdah (3,207 metres). As this region has a much higher rainfall than the rest of the country, it has denser vegetation and during the MONSOON rains has many seasonal rivers and waterfalls. The Tihamah Plain lies between the Asir highlands and the coast.

Behind the Hejaz, to the east, lies the plateau of Najd, which is covered in deep gullies made by the wind and tropical rains. Some mountain ranges here rise to 500 metres above the plateau. The Najd slopes towards low-lying plains in the east. This region was once the bed of an ancient sea, shrunk by climatic change, which survives today as the shallow Arabian Gulf. Along the Gulf coast there is a wide zone of salt flats, tidal marshes and, here and there, MANGROVE swamps.

To the north and south of this eastern plain are two of the great hot deserts of the world. In the north, the Nafud is a flat, stony expanse covering 57,000 square kilometres. In south-east Saudi Arabia lies the formidable sand desert of al-Rub' al-Khali ("the Empty Quarter"), an area of 650,000 square kilometres. These two deserts are linked by a 1,300-kilometre arc of shifting sandy desert called al-Dahna.

In all of Saudi Arabia there are only two natural fresh-water lakes, at Laila in the central Tuwaiq Mountains, and there are no permanent rivers. Dry gullies (WADIS) channel water after rain storms.

The most typical natural vegetation is low-growing thorn bush and scrub. The dusty scene is varied by oases — green and fertile areas around natural springs and wells which can range in size from a few hectares to many square kilometres. The biggest are north of Riyadh (at Hail and Buraidah), south of the city (al-Kharj) and in the eastern region (at Hufuf, and Qatif). These and other oases have been developed using modern agricultural methods.

◄An oasis at Hail in the northern Najd, near the Nafud Desert. Dates and vegetables are grown on fertile land around permanent springs at the foot of arid mountain ranges.

▲Mountains of the Hejaz, near Jeddah. Black volcanic rock of hardened lava is covered with a drifting layer of sand.

Most of Saudi Arabia is very dry, with great extremes of temperature. The little rain that does fall is scarce and erratic.

The country lies between the weather systems of the Mediterranean and the Tropics. The north-westerly winter rains from the Mediterranean affect the northern Hejaz, but weaken as they cross the mountains and reach the Nafud. At higher altitudes the winter brings frost and even snow.

At this time too, a dry north-east wind called the SHAMAL crosses the country. The sand it carries falls as a haze of brown dust which finds its way into every nook and cranny, even indoors.

Between May and October the winds shift to the south-west and blow strongly, carrying moist air picked up from the Indian Ocean. The greatest amount of rain falls in the high Asir (480 mm a year). Further east,

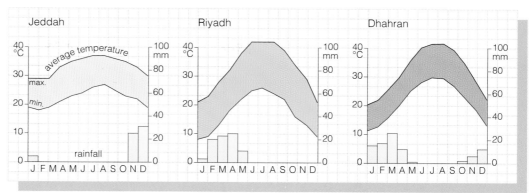

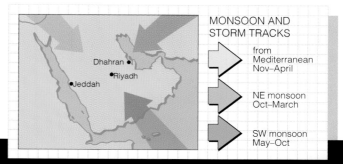

▲ *Temperatures on the coast do not reach as high as in the interior, but at sea level the atmosphere is much more humid.*

◄ *After a rain storm, floods drain into a wadi, providing temporary surface water.*

MONSOON AND STORM TRACKS

from Mediterranean Nov–April

NE monsoon Oct–March

SW monsoon May–Oct

◄ *The pool of cool blue water among these dunes is not real — it is a mirage caused by extreme heat.*

KEY FACTS

● The highest temperature recorded in Saudi Arabia is 54°C.
● The Tropic of Cancer passes through Saudi Arabia south of Medina, so the sun is directly overhead at noon on 21 June.

these monsoon clouds evaporate as they rise over the mountains along the border with Yemen and Oman. Most of the rain they carry falls on the southern slopes of the mountains. If the monsoons do push northwards, the rain comes in heavy thunderstorms, but the supply is unreliable and therefore of little use to farmers. The country's average annual rainfall is 30–100 mm, but in most areas outside Asir Province 10 or even 20 years' drought is not unusual.

The cloudless skies over central Saudi Arabia mean that there are extremes of temperature. Daytime temperatures are very high, averaging 30°C and often reaching over 40°C in summer, but the temperature plummets after sunset. It is not unusual to experience a range of 40°C in one day. In summer, Riyadh is so hot that the government moves to the cooler mountain town of Taif, in the Hejaz. But in winter, morning frost in Riyadh is common.

On the coasts humidity is higher, making the more moderate temperatures there feel uncomfortable.

NATURAL RESOURCES

Below the deserts of Saudi Arabia lie huge reservoirs of its most precious natural resources: water and oil. Water is very scarce, because more than 90% of the land receives no regular rainfall. There are no permanent rivers to provide supplies of water and feed lakes.

However, since ancient times desert people have made use of FOSSIL WATER. This forms when rain falls and filters through the ground until it is trapped by a "waterproof" layer of rock. The water then spreads out. Where the rock dips into a saucer shape, the water collects in a pool. Over thousands of years, rain falling on the

▼ *Drilling for oil in the desert in Eastern Province.*

Hejaz Mountains has been trapped underground in this way.

Where the water appears at the surface naturally, springs form and oases develop. The biggest oases in Saudi Arabia are at al-Hasa and north and south of Riyadh, in Eastern Province. The largest springs appear at two lakes at Laila. Where the water is near enough to the surface, it can be reached by digging wells. These can be between seven and 15 metres deep if dug by hand, but with modern equipment water can be pumped from a depth of hundreds of metres.

Oil and gas, formed many millions of years ago from decaying animal and plant matter, were trapped underground in much

OIL RESERVES
(1992, billion barrels)

Saudi Arabia	257.8
Iraq	100
Kuwait	94
Iran	92.9
Abu Dhabi (UAE)	92.2
Venezuela	59.1
former USSR	57
Mexico	51.3
USA	26.3
China	24
UK	3.9

▼ *Saudi Arabia's climate is ideal for solar power, but so far there are only experimental projects, like the one below.*

▶ *Riyadh depends on water piped from DESALINATION plants on the east coast. Its water tower is a landmark.*

the same way as water. Saudi Arabia has the biggest oil reserves in the world, a quarter of the world's known reserves of 991,000 million barrels. The country's oil fields lie under the eastern plain and the Arabian Gulf. This whole region is rich in oil.

Other natural resources in Saudi Arabia include large deposits of iron ore, and smaller quantities of copper, gold and zinc. However, there has been little interest in developing these, because it would not be profitable.

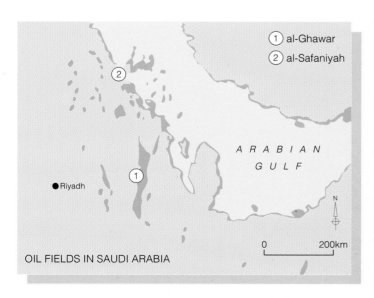

① al-Ghawar
② al-Safaniyah

ARABIAN GULF

● Riyadh

N

0   200km

OIL FIELDS IN SAUDI ARABIA

KEY FACTS

● Fossil water used to irrigate fields at al-Hasa is 17,000 years old.
● There are fresh-water springs on the bed of the Arabian Gulf.
● Oil is measured in "barrels" (bbls) and production in "barrels a day" (bpd).
● There are only 37 "supergiant" oil fields in the world, each with over 5,000 million barrels of oil. Saudi Arabia has 11, including the world's biggest onshore and offshore fields (al-Ghawar and al-Safaniyah).

POPULATION

The people who live in Saudi Arabia fall into two separate groups: about 12 million are Saudi nationals, and some 4.5 million are EXPATRIATES — foreigners who are allowed to live there to work.

TRADITIONAL LIFE-STYLES
Most Saudis in the interior used to live in villages, farming at oases and in fertile wadis. Others lived as nomadic herders. The Bedouin (which means "desert dwellers") herded camels, goats and sheep, moving their camps with the seasons to give their animals the best available feeding and water supplies. In the hottest months they moved to the edge of the oases, where they traded their products, such as leather, for goods from the towns and villages.

In the towns, especially along the coasts, there were many prosperous merchants and craftsmen. They lived by trading with the interior, with other regions of Arabia, or even with East Africa and India.

SAUDI ARABIA TODAY
Since the 1960s, Saudis have increasingly left their traditional way of life. Now 73% work in the fast-growing towns and cities, for example in business, government administration and the armed forces. Those who remain in the countryside have also changed their life-style, because they can afford radios, kerosene stoves, vehicles and small luxuries. Today few Bedouin

◄ *The bazaar (SOUK) in Jeddah is always busy. Traditional merchants' houses, four or five storeys high, were built from coral rock and teak. Carved wooden screens at the window allow women to watch the street below without being seen.*

◄ *It is a Bedouin custom to offer coffee to a guest and an insult to refuse it. In the towns, coffee houses are a favourite place for men to sit and relax.*

▼ *This Saudi family is strolling down a street in Jeddah. But in stricter areas, such as Riyadh, a woman could not appear in public with her face uncovered.*

KEY FACTS

● Saudi Arabia has the world's third highest population growth rate – 5.6%. At this rate the population will double by the year 2006.

● Riyadh has the world's highest urban expansion rate: its population has grown 500% in 20 years.

● In 1992 the biggest group of pilgrims came from Indonesia (125,000), followed by Iran (116,000) and Pakistan (87,000).

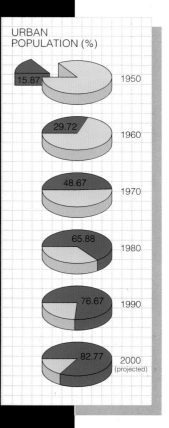

URBAN POPULATION (%)

15.87	1950
29.72	1960
48.67	1970
65.88	1980
76.67	1990
82.77	2000 (projected)

POPULATION

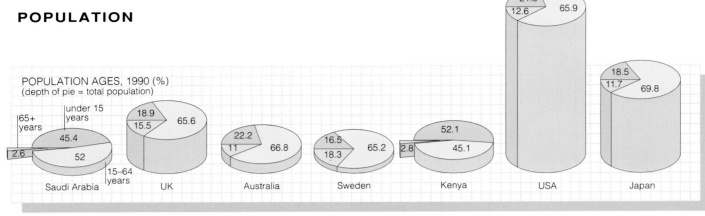

POPULATION AGES, 1990 (%)
(depth of pie = total population)

65+ years | under 15 years

Saudi Arabia: 45.4 / 52 / 2.6 — 15–64 years
UK: 18.9 / 15.5 / 65.6
Australia: 22.2 / 11 / 66.8
Sweden: 16.5 / 18.3 / 65.2
Kenya: 52.1 / 45.1 / 2.8
USA: 21.5 / 12.6 / 65.9
Japan: 18.5 / 11.7 / 69.8

depend on a nomadic existence.

But some traditions remain very strong. People's names immediately show their tribe and family line, and there are strong regional and family loyalties. Islam and Arabic are the common bond between all Saudis.

In the remote south-western Asir, people have distinctive traditions — different houses, clothing and culture. Women here do not wear the veil. Their traditional dress includes wide-brimmed straw hats with high crowns.

EXPATRIATES AND PILGRIMS
Foreigners who work in Saudi Arabia are only permitted to enter the country on temporary contracts. They cannot remain

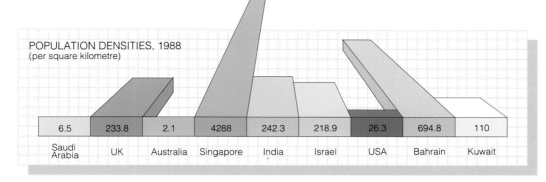

POPULATION DENSITIES, 1988
(per square kilometre)

Saudi Arabia	UK	Australia	Singapore	India	Israel	USA	Bahrain	Kuwait
6.5	233.8	2.1	4288	242.3	218.9	26.3	694.8	110

◀ *Almost half of all Saudis are aged under 15.*

▶ *Saudi Arabia's water resources are scarce, but there is no pressure on land.*

permanently. Some are highly qualified professionals, such as engineers, architects, doctors and bankers. Many more are unskilled labourers. Expatriate workers from the Philippines alone (400,000) provide 15% of all domestic servants and more than 50% of all hospital staff in Saudi Arabia.

Each year up to 2 million Moslems of more than 70 nationalities come to Saudi Arabia on pilgrimage. For several weeks the government must provide shelter (mainly tents), water, food, medical, transport and other services for pilgrims staying outside Mecca — the equivalent of setting up a city the size of Barcelona where the inhabitants do not speak a common language.

◀ *Thai and Filipino construction workers in Jubail. Saudi Arabia's modernization could not have been achieved without the millions of expatriates who have worked there.*

▶ *Expatriates relax at the weekend with a barbecue around the pool in their own accommodation complex.*

RELIGION

Islam, the religion of Saudi Arabia, has many rules for public and private behaviour, as well as religious duties. All non-Moslems in the country must also follow some of these rules.

The working week runs from Saturday morning to Thursday midday and during the week offices close at prayer times. Moslems obey the MUEZZIN's call to prayer five times daily: at dawn, noon, mid-afternoon, sunset and evening. People pray in the mosque or in public places, always facing towards Mecca. The main prayer gathering is at noon on Friday, the Moslem holy day. Exact times of sunrise, sunset and the new moon appear in Saudi newspapers.

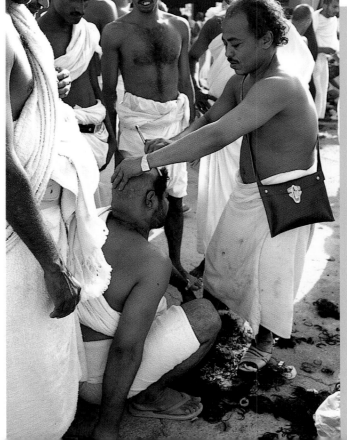

EDUCATION

Education is an important part of Islam. Boys especially must learn by heart the Koran, the holy book, and learn the "Hadith" (traditions). They attend special schools (MADRASSAH) where they are given Koranic teaching.

Schooling is free and available to everyone. Boys and girls are educated separately. When the first state girls' school opened in 1963 many people complained to the King. The first college was opened in 1958. Now renamed the University of Riyadh, it has separate men's and women's campuses, with a total of some 20,000 students. Today there are other universities and colleges too, including a University of Petroleum and Minerals at Dhahran. Many male students continue specialist training overseas.

◀*These worshippers are in the Prophet's Mosque at Medina, which is being extended to hold 257,000 people. The Great Mosque, Mecca, holds 1 million.*

◀HAJ *pilgrims wear seamless white robes so as not to display differences in wealth or nationality. After Id al-Adha, they shave their heads as a sign of purity.*

THE ISLAMIC CALENDAR AND FESTIVALS

The Islamic calendar starts from AD 16 July 622, when the Prophet Mohammed left Mecca for Medina. The Islamic year has 12 lunar months, which start when the new moon appears, totalling 354 days. Each day starts at sunset precisely and runs until the next sunset. Friday is the holy day and day of rest.

The only public holidays in Saudi Arabia are religious festivals. These include 10 days at Id al-Fitr at the end of Ramadan, the month of fasting, and 4 days at Id al-Adha, the tenth day of the month of the haj. New Year is the first of the month of Muharram.

1 January 1994	19 Rajab 1414
9 June 1994	1 Muharram 1415
30 May 1995	1 Muharram 1416
19 May 1996	1 Muharram 1417

▼*Saudi schoolchildren are still taught by traditional methods, learning the Koran by heart. Expatriate children go to different schools.*

KEY FACTS

● Correct behaviour is enforced by the religious police (MUTAWA), who patrol the streets and even enter private houses to check on people.
● In 1958 Saudi Arabia had only 20 primary schools, but by 1987 it had over 10,500.
● The Arabic language is written from right to left.
● Gambling and alcohol are forbidden throughout Saudi Arabia.

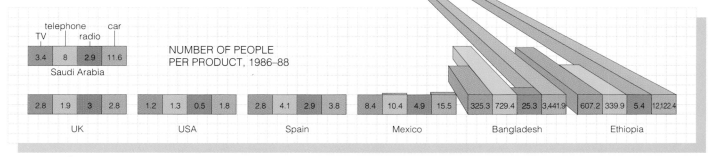

	TV	telephone	radio	car	
Saudi Arabia	3.4	8	2.9	11.6	NUMBER OF PEOPLE PER PRODUCT, 1986–88
UK	2.8	1.9	3	2.8	
USA	1.2	1.3	0.5	1.8	
Spain	2.8	4.1	2.9	3.8	
Mexico	8.4	10.4	4.9	15.5	
Bangladesh	325.3	729.4	25.3	3,441.9	
Ethiopia	607.2	339.9	5.4	12,122.4	

▲ *Saudis can afford to buy many imported goods.*

▶ *This Saudi home is decorated with colourful carpets and local craftwork. Women live in a separate section of the house.*

▲ *Jewellery in the gold souk is sold by weight, at prices that are updated daily. Sales are worth around $1,300 million a year.*

HOME LIFE

In Islam, a man may have up to four wives, so a large family of half-brothers and half-sisters and their mothers may all live in one house. At home, Saudi girls and women have separate living rooms and bedrooms, and do not eat with the men and boys. In the street or at work, a female must follow certain strict rules: she must not speak to a man, or even sit beside him, unless he is a member of her family. She must cover her hair, arms and legs in public with a long cloak, though she may be wearing jeans or a designer dress underneath. In the strictest areas (like Riyadh) she must also cover her face with a veil or mask. Expatriate women often wear cloaks in public too.

Saudi men and boys wear simple long cotton robes, and a loose head-dress held in place by a black rope-like band. This national dress is the same for all, with little difference for rich and poor, although there are regional variations. It is a practical and comfortable way to dress and shield the head from the hot sun. But at home, or when overseas, men often wear the same jeans or business suits as those around them.

RETAIL PRICES, 1989 (US $)

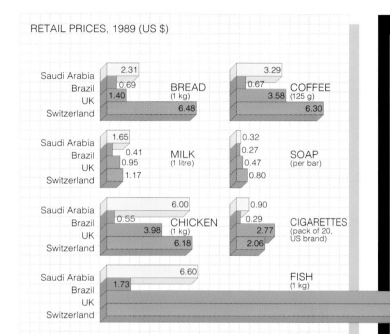

KEY FACTS

● In Islam the left hand is considered unclean, so it is never used in greeting or to pass something.
● Saudi parents arrange the marriages of their sons and daughters.
● Saudi Arabia has the highest rate of death from diabetes in the world: 60 people die from it each day.
● The first McDonald's in Saudi Arabia opened in 1993.

▶ *Saudi health services have some of the most advanced hospitals in the world, but most medical staff are foreign. King Faisal Hospital in Riyadh is one of the best hospitals in the Middle East. However, many Bedouin still prefer to use traditional medicine.*

► *The coast road in Jeddah has been decorated with many fun sculptures. Saudi and expatriate families enjoy the beach, but Saudi women and girls do not wear swimsuits in public.*

LEISURE

Traditional leisure activities are hunting with falcons or dogs, and horse and camel racing. Football and water sports are also popular now. People in towns enjoy picnics in the desert at weekends — either just for the day or camping in Bedouin style. Films and television programmes are strictly censored to conform with Islam, but Arabic music is heard everywhere.

Islam forbids drunkenness, and all alcohol is banned in the country, so there are no pubs, discos or bars, even in hotels. The traditional drink is coffee. There are harsh punishments for importing alcohol, drugs and certain videos or books. The same rules apply to expatriates.

◄ *The King's Camel Race is held in April or May, near Riyadh. Thousands of camels take part in the 19-km race through the desert, for big prize money. The jockeys are young boys who make sure they stay the course by fixing Velcro to the saddle!*

RULE AND LAW

Saudi Arabia is an Islamic monarchy. The ruling Saud family belongs to the strict Wahhabi branch of Islam, which was founded in Najd. The King is titled the Custodian of the Two Holy Places, because this is his greatest duty. He is also the country's IMAM, or religious leader. The traditional form of government among Bedouin Arabs is the MAJLIS — an open meeting where all subjects can plead their case. The King still holds majlis, as do local tribal leaders.

The country is not a democracy: there are no political parties, no-one can vote and there is no Parliament. The King (who is also Prime Minister) and his Council of Ministers

► **King Fahd is descended from Ibn Saud, who unified the kingdom in 1932.**

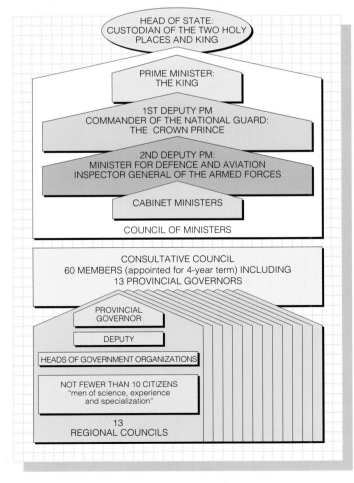

HEAD OF STATE: CUSTODIAN OF THE TWO HOLY PLACES AND KING
PRIME MINISTER: THE KING
1ST DEPUTY PM COMMANDER OF THE NATIONAL GUARD: THE CROWN PRINCE
2ND DEPUTY PM: MINISTER FOR DEFENCE AND AVIATION INSPECTOR GENERAL OF THE ARMED FORCES
CABINET MINISTERS
COUNCIL OF MINISTERS

CONSULTATIVE COUNCIL
60 MEMBERS (appointed for 4-year term) INCLUDING 13 PROVINCIAL GOVERNORS

PROVINCIAL GOVERNOR
DEPUTY
HEADS OF GOVERNMENT ORGANIZATIONS
NOT FEWER THAN 10 CITIZENS "men of science, experience and specialization"
13 REGIONAL COUNCILS

▲ **"There is no god but God; and Mohammed is His Messenger". These words from the Koran appear on the Saudi flag, together with a traditional Arabian sword.**

27

agree all government decisions. The two Deputy Prime Ministers (who are also members of the royal family) head the armed forces, which are among the best equipped in the Middle East.

Saudi social, political and economic law is based on the Islamic SHARIAH and courts have religious judges (QADI). Crimes such as theft, adultery and murder carry harsh penalties, including execution. The crime rate is low.

After the Gulf War in 1990–91, the Saudi King announced political reforms. In 1993 the 60-member Consultative Council was created, to review decisions made by the government.

▼ *In August 1990 Iraq invaded Kuwait. Saudi forces fought alongside troops from the USA, Britain and other countries to drive the invaders out in February 1991. Here Saudi air force jets patrol the desert during the war.*

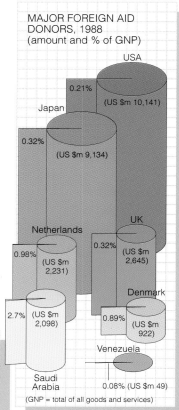

MAJOR FOREIGN AID DONORS, 1988 (amount and % of GNP)

USA 0.21% (US $m 10,141)
Japan 0.32% (US $m 9,134)
Netherlands 0.98% (US $m 2,231)
UK 0.32% (US $m 2,645)
Denmark 0.89% (US $m 922)
Saudi Arabia 2.7% (US $m 2,098)
Venezuela 0.08% (US $m 49)

(GNP = total of all goods and services)

KEY FACTS

● Saudi Arabia is one of the few countries in the world called after a family.
● Non-Moslems are barred from the holy cities of Mecca and Medina.
● Slavery in Saudi Arabia was abolished in 1961.
● Trading in drugs can result in the death penalty.

DEFENCE SPENDING, 1992 (US $ per head of population)

Brazil	9
India	9
China	19
Pakistan	27
Argentina	43
Japan	136
UK	366
France	385
USA	964
Saudi Arabia	1,371

FOOD AND FARMING

Farming in Saudi Arabia used to be limited by lack of water and fertile soil. In the south-west, where the climate is best suited to growing crops, the steep hillsides were terraced to make fields for wheat, coffee and other produce. In the arid north and east, only the areas around oases could be cultivated. Some villages still use ancient IRRIGATION systems, with modern improvements like electric water pumps.

Since the mid-1980s, farming has developed fast. In 1991 some 1.8 million hectares of land were under cultivation, nearly twice the area in 1986.

On small farms, vegetables, dates and other fruit remain the chief crops. Large

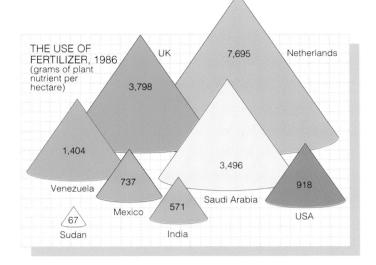

THE USE OF FERTILIZER, 1986 (grams of plant nutrient per hectare)

UK 3,798
Netherlands 7,695
Venezuela 1,404
Saudi Arabia 3,496
Mexico 737
India 571
USA 918
Sudan 67

▼ *Water for irrigation comes from fossil water and coastal desalination plants. These fields are circular so that a rotating sprinkler can reach the whole area.*

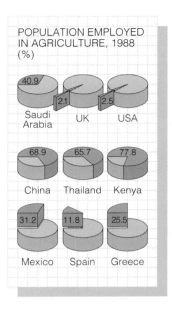

◀ Fishing in coastal waters provides half the country's needs. Oil pollution in the Gulf in 1991 reduced the local shrimp catch to 1% of the level before the Gulf War and destroyed exports to Japan and the USA.

POPULATION EMPLOYED IN AGRICULTURE, 1988 (%)

40.9 Saudi Arabia	2.1 UK	2.5 USA
68.9 China	65.7 Thailand	77.8 Kenya
31.2 Mexico	11.8 Spain	25.5 Greece

farms use techniques that include precisely controlled irrigation systems, pesticides, chemical fertilizer, drought- and disease-resistant crops and new cultivation methods, such as HYDROPONICS. This has brought dramatic results: the wheat harvest increased from 142,000 tonnes in 1979/80 to 3.9 million tonnes in 1990/1. That year 1.7 million tonnes were exported. Other crops whose yields have increased are barley, maize and ALFALFA, which are used for fodder.

The biggest farming projects are in Eastern Province, around the ancient oases of Hufuf and Qatif, and north of Riyadh. By planting TAMARISK trees and grasses to stop the soil blowing away, thousands of hectares of farmland have been reclaimed from the desert. Farmers receive large subsidies from the government – free water, cheap electricity and tax benefits. The government buys home-grown wheat at six times the price on world markets.

Saudi Arabia produces all its own dairy produce. Dairy cattle are reared intensively near Riyadh. The biggest poultry farm in the Middle East is in Eastern Province.

KEY FACTS

● Saudi Arabia has 12 million date palms. 29% of the annual 500,000-tonne date harvest comes from the Riyadh area.
● Saudi Arabia is the world's biggest buyer of live sheep (about 6 million in 1991).
● The country is the sixth biggest exporter of wheat (after the USA, Canada, the European Union, Australia and Argentina).
● Saudi Arabia is the biggest consumer of broiler chickens in the world – 40 kilos per person per year.

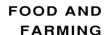

◀ Dates have been grown in Arabia for 4,000 years. The date palm needs less water than any other crop. A tree can produce fruit for up to 200 years and can yield up to 100 kilos of dates a year.

▶ Breaking the daily fast of Ramadan after sunset with a traditional meal. The women of the household eat separately.

The country still imports much food, including processed food from Europe and America, which is popular mainly with expatriates. American-style fast food and international restaurants are available in the cities, but traditional food remains the Saudi favourite.

A celebration feast includes rice with nuts and raisins, houmus (a paste made from beans), pitta bread and tabullah salad (made with cracked wheat, mint and parsley). The main dish is a whole roasted lamb. People often eat with their fingers, sharing dishes. Dates and sweet tea are popular snacks.

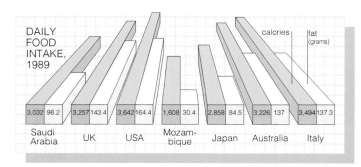

DAILY FOOD INTAKE, 1989

calories | fat (grams)

	Saudi Arabia	UK	USA	Mozambique	Japan	Australia	Italy
calories	3,032	3,257	3,642	1,608	2,858	3,226	3,494
fat (grams)	98.2	143.4	164.4	30.4	84.5	137	137.3

TRADE AND INDUSTRY

THE OIL INDUSTRY

The Saudi economy is based almost totally on oil – producing crude oil and refining it into different products. Some of these are fuels, like petrol and kerosene. Others (petrochemicals) are raw materials for industry.

Oil was first discovered in Saudi Arabia in the 1930s by American oil companies, who were allowed to produce it in exchange for giving a percentage of their earnings to the government. In the 1960s and 1970s, most oil came from Arab countries. They forced the price up so that foreign oil companies would make better agreements with them. However, in the 1980s new sources (like

▼ *The petrochemicals industry processes oil and gas to make chemicals used in everyday products such as plastics and fertilizer.*

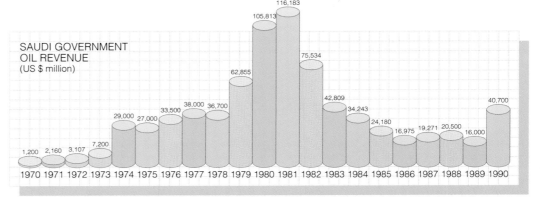

SAUDI GOVERNMENT OIL REVENUE (US $ million)

Year	Revenue
1970	1,200
1971	2,160
1972	3,107
1973	7,200
1974	29,000
1975	27,000
1976	33,500
1977	38,000
1978	36,700
1979	62,855
1980	105,813
1981	116,183
1982	75,534
1983	42,809
1984	34,243
1985	24,180
1986	16,975
1987	19,271
1988	20,500
1989	16,000
1990	40,700

Alaska and the North Sea) came into production and the price dropped. Today, oil prices are fairly stable.

Saudi Aramco is now responsible for all oil production in Saudi Arabia. Its headquarters are at Dhahran. The country's seven oil refineries are at Ras Tanura and Jubail on the Gulf, Yanbu (two refineries), Jeddah and Rabigh on the Red Sea, and Riyadh.

DEVELOPMENT

The Saudi government has used the billions of dollars it has earned from oil to modernize the country's facilities and services: building roads, airports, hospitals, schools, housing, water supplies and telecommunications services. Since the late 1970s it has even built two new industrial cities – Jubail on the Gulf coast and Yanbu on the Red Sea coast, with populations planned to reach 100,000 by the year 2000.

The government has drawn up a series of

TRADE AND INDUSTRY

◀ *Crude and refined oil products are exported from Ras Tanura, where a refinery processes 520,000 barrels of oil a day.*

KEY FACTS

● Oil cost $3 a barrel in 1973, $30 in 1981 and $16 in 1993.

● By 2000, Saudi Arabia will be able to refine 50% of its oil production.

● All companies in the country must be owned mainly by the government or Saudi nationals.

● Saudi Arabia imports all its aviation fuel.

● Industrial exports (apart from oil and gas, fertilizer and petrochemicals) increased by 15% in 1992.

● Saudi Arabia's biggest trading partners are the USA, Britain and Japan for imports, and the USA, Singapore and France for exports.

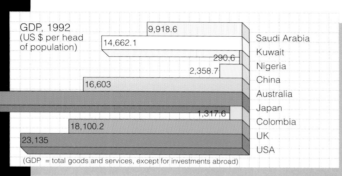

GDP, 1992
(US $ per head of population)

9,918.6	Saudi Arabia
14,662.1	Kuwait
290.6	Nigeria
2,358.7	China
16,603	Australia
29,376.6	Japan
1,317.6	Colombia
18,100.2	UK
23,135	USA

(GDP = total goods and services, except for investments abroad)

▼ *The Red Sea fishing port of Yanbu is developing into a major new industrial city.*

plans for development and has set up organizations to co-ordinate different projects. For example, Saudi Basic Industries Corporation plans and invests in petrochemical companies which process natural gas. It employs 10,000 people in Saudi Arabia and overseas. One of its latest projects is to build a polyester fibre plant at Yanbu to supply the carpet and bottling industries.

Since oil prices have dropped, Saudi Arabia has agreed barter deals where it pays for goods and services with oil instead of money. Other trade deals make overseas companies re-invest part of their profits in Saudi Arabia, or provide technical

▲ *More Saudi nationals are replacing foreign staff in professional and technical jobs.*

◀ *The business district in central Riyadh. Banking and insurance are important services. Women have separate banking facilities.*

assistance. For example, recently a French company that wanted a defence contract agreed to help a local company establish a gold-refining plant.

OTHER INDUSTRIES
Apart from oil, other industries are centred on the ports of Jeddah, Qatif and Dammam, as well as Riyadh. Major products are metals, construction materials like cement, and foodstuffs such as vegetable oil and milk powder.

Another very important industry is the desalination of seawater, for both irrigation and domestic use. There are 15 desalination plants, which produce 500 million gallons of water a day – 70% of the country's needs. Capacity will be doubled by the year 2000. These plants also generate 20% of Saudi Arabia's electric power.

TRANSPORT

◄ *For centuries camels (called "the ships of the desert") provided transport for Arabs and their goods. Now four-wheel-drive vehicles do their job.*

▼ *Two-thirds of haj pilgrims arrive by air, at a rate of a flight a minute at the busiest time of year. This transit area at Jeddah's King Abdul-Aziz Airport can shelter up to 600,000 people.*

Travel in Saudi Arabia has changed dramatically in recent years. Many families now have more than one car and there are over 2 million cars in the kingdom. Driving is undisciplined and more than 20,000 people are killed on the roads each year. Women are not allowed to drive. They usually travel with a private driver or by taxi. Bus services link Saudi towns and neighbouring states but are used mainly by migrant workers. There are plans to build a light railway in the Mecca area, to make travel easier for pilgrims. A 900-kilometre railway linking the Gulf ports and Riyadh is used mainly for freight.

Since 1980, new international airports have been built in Jeddah, Riyadh, Dhahran

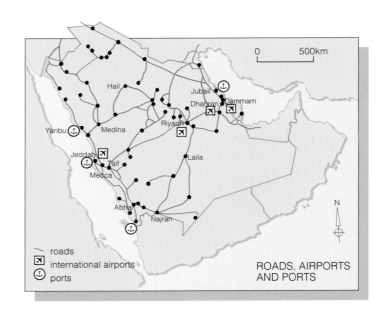

ROADS, AIRPORTS AND PORTS

roads
international airports
ports

and Dammam. Saudia, the national airline, has a fleet of 111 aircraft and carried 11.5 million passengers on domestic and international routes in 1992.

Oil and gas are pumped from the well-head to the loading terminal or refinery through a network of pipelines. The giant new 1,200-kilometre Petroline pumps 5 million barrels of oil and gas a day from Jubail on the east coast to Yanbu on the west. This saves tankers from having to travel round the Arabian coast before going on to Europe or America — the pipeline cuts 3,500 kilometres off the journey. By 1995 Saudi Arabia will have a fleet of 25 supertankers.

▲ *There are 122,000 km of modern roads in Saudi Arabia.*

▼ *Saudis rely on private cars and taxis for transport in the modern city centres.*

KEY FACTS

● Petrol in Saudi Arabia is the cheapest in the world – about US $0.10 a gallon.
● Riyadh has the highest average urban traffic speed in the world (43 kph).
● King Khaled International Airport at Riyadh is the biggest in the world (185 square kilometres).
● About 300,000 private drivers are employed in Saudi Arabia.

THE ENVIRONMENT

The desert is harsh for human life, but many animals, birds and plants are adapted to its conditions. For example, the camel has a unique ability to survive in the desert. It can walk quickly (8–16 kph), using little energy, and can live for ten or 15 days at temperatures of 30–35°C without drinking. But then it will take in 100 litres of water at one go! Camels also eat thorn bush and other unappetising vegetation. Even their eyes have special protection against the frequent blinding sand storms.

Other mammals in Saudi Arabia include many types of gazelle and members of the cat family — from mountain leopards to tiny sand-cats (ancestor of our domestic tabbies). There are baboons, wolves, foxes and mongooses too. Reptiles include scorpions, lizards and snakes, such as cobras, sidewinders and vipers. Locusts (migrating from East Africa) and mosquitos used to be a problem, but today their numbers have been limited by pesticides.

In the early part of the 20th century, hunting with automatic rifles was a popular activity. This severely reduced the numbers of game animals in Saudi Arabia, and some became extinct. Now only two traditional kinds of hunting are allowed: falconry and COURSING with the Arabian hunting dog, the saluki.

The country's coastal waters and islands are home to many different creatures.

▼ *In 1991 the shallow tidal zone of the Arabian Gulf was invaded by sticky black crude oil. Damage still continues.*

Those of the Red Sea include giant moray eels and manta rays. A ray can have a wing span of 5 metres and weigh several tonnes. Fish to watch out for are stonefish, which have poisonous spines, and stinging lionfish. DUGONGS, whales and dolphins are found in the Gulf as well as the Red Sea. The shallow coastal waters of the Gulf also contain oyster beds, whose pearls are among the best in the world. They have been harvested for thousands of years. Some 90% of Saudi Arabia's turtles breed on the offshore coral islands.

The greatest risk of pollution in Saudi Arabia is from accidental oil spillages. The equivalent of 250,000 barrels of oil are spilled into the Gulf each year. Burning off gas at oil well-heads releases carbon dioxide into the atmosphere. However, because Saudi crude oil has a relatively low sulphur content, and there is little rainfall, there is less risk of acid rain.

During the Gulf War in 1991, when oil storage tanks on the coast of Kuwait exploded, there was a near catastrophe. About 3–4 million barrels of oil were

KEY FACTS

● Over 6,000 million migrating birds fly over or visit Saudi Arabia each year.
● The rare rheem gazelle may spend its whole life without drinking water. It finds moisture in plants and by licking dew off its coat.
● The "desert shrimp" grows, mates and dies within a few days in the pools left after rain storms. The eggs wait up to 20 years for the next rain before growing.
● Sea snakes in the Arabian Gulf are among the world's deadliest. One drop of their venom could kill five adults.
● The camel was domesticated in Arabia 4,000 years ago and the saluki 8,000 years ago.
● With Saudi help, the native Arabian oryx was re-introduced into the wild in 1980. Before then, it had survived only in captivity.

◀ *The Arabian mountain leopard, one of 16 endangered native mammals. Lions disappeared in the middle of the 19th century, ostriches became extinct in the 1930s, and the last wild cheetah was shot in 1973.*

◀ *Falconry requires great skill. Falconers train young hawks to fly free to attack their prey, and then return to the falconer's wrist.*

released into the sea and the slick spread 430 kilometres south-east along the Saudi coast as far as Dammam. Half the oil evaporated, the equivalent of 300,000 barrels was recovered and the rest sank down to the sea bed. About 20,000 seabirds died, while unknown numbers of fish and other marine life were destroyed or

contaminated. The long-term effects on marine life are still not certain. One positive result was that rescuers cleared rubbish from the offshore coral islands, and now their turtle populations have increased.

Ground water accumulated over thousands of years has been heavily used for irrigation and drinking water in the eastern region. This has reduced supplies in some places. A new danger is the heavy use of fertilizer, which can contaminate the ground water. The soil can also be ruined by excessive watering, which forms a crust of mineral salts on the surface. But one positive effect of increased watering has been more bird life, especially in the east. Birds migrating for the winter, from central Asia to Africa and from northern Europe to India, break their long journeys in Saudi Arabia. The number of bird species found at pools of treated sewage water in al-Hair

◀ *The northern Red Sea contains some spectacular coral gardens. Special conditions let the 177 coral species grow at some of the fastest rates recorded, up to 39 centimetres a year.*

▲ *A modern shopping mall contrasts with the natural environment – cool and shaded from the glaring sun – but depends on electric power for light, air-conditioning and an escalator.*

reserve, south of Riyadh, has increased from 90 to 270 in ten years.

Since the 1980s, the government has been encouraging conservation. By 1995 there should be 56 wildlife reserves and 52 marine area reserves throughout the country. The most important reserve is the mountainous National Park of the Asir, covering 4,500 square kilometres. This region is the richest in wildlife. It also contains remote areas of special interest: above the 1,800-metre line, juniper forests and other plants match the plant life of northern Greece, thousands of kilometres

away. They are survivors from the region's cooler climate during the last Ice Age. Tourism is growing in all these areas.

Riyadh Zoo, created in 1987, is world-class. It houses 1,400 animals of 350 different species. These include endangered native creatures such as the houbara bustard, the griffon vulture and the sand-cat, and others such as brown bears and ostriches which are extinct in the wild in Saudi Arabia. The zoo also conserves rare species like the Arabian leopard, the cheetah and the bataleur eagle.

Environmental awareness in Saudi Arabia has been slow to increase. Lead-free petrol will be available in 1995, but household waste materials are not recycled. Rubbish is collected under contract to overseas companies; the work is done by foreign labourers.

THE FUTURE

Within three generations Saudi Arabia has been transformed. Its huge oil wealth has been used to create modern services to which all its people have free access. Many Saudi families today enjoy a luxury standard of living.

This rapid change has only been possible by hiring foreign experts and labourers to work in the country, and by importing all the necessary equipment and high technology. The only income Saudi Arabia has to pay for all this comes from selling oil.

In recent years the price of oil has fallen, to about half of its peak price in 1981. The price is not likely to rise to such a high level again. New sources of oil and gas — for example, in Siberia and Vietnam — will become easily available to the industrialized countries which buy most fuel. If Saudi Arabia's income falls, its development plans will have to become more modest.

Because the Middle East has been the scene of many political and religious disputes, Saudi Arabia (like other oil producers in the region) has had to build strong defence forces. Its export routes pass through the Gulf and the Red Sea, which are both vulnerable areas. Already Saudi Arabia spends about a third of its budget on military equipment and armed forces. Iraq's invasion of Kuwait in 1990 is a reminder of the dangers in the region.

If government spending has to drop, certain social changes will speed up. The country's strict rules of behaviour are being challenged more and more. Already educated Saudis are filling more jobs previously held by expatriates. Educated women especially

KEY FACTS

● In 1989 over 400 people died when the Great Mosque at Mecca was besieged by Iranians who demanded control of the holy places.
● In 1990 42 Saudi women protesters drove around Riyadh illegally for about half an hour before they were arrested. They were soon released.
● In 1985 Prince Sultan Ibn Sulman became the first Arab, the first Moslem and the first member of royalty to go on a space mission.

▶ *Some Saudi women who hold qualifications already have jobs. In the future they will ask for more choice and recognition in their careers.*

are beginning to want to follow careers that they have been trained for. Many Saudis have travelled overseas, have seen foreign films and now have satellite television, so they are meeting new ideas and different ways of living.

The future of Saudi Arabia may also change when the Arab countries reach a final peace with Israel. The first steps towards this were taken in September 1993. If there is a lasting peace, there will be new opportunities for development. Perhaps the old pipeline for exporting Saudi oil from the Mediterranean will reopen, and there will be prosperous trade between countries in the region.

One danger is that the old enemy Israel will be replaced by new threats. For example, extreme Moslem groups in Iran have made it clear they they want to control the holy places in Saudi Arabia.

Although Saudi oil reserves will last for 100 years at the present rate of production – that is, for about five generations – it is not easy to know whether or not the future will be peaceful and prosperous. The answer depends partly on people in the rest of the world. Will we continue to use oil and gas at the same ever increasing rate that we do now?

▼ *Pipelines pump oil and gas across scorching sandy wastes. The deserts of Saudi Arabia will remain long after its underground resources run out.*

FURTHER INFORMATION

ISLAM

Islam was founded in the land that is now Saudi Arabia in the 7th century. Moslems believe that the Prophet Mohammed received God's message from the Angel Gabriel, and that he was the last in a line of prophets which started with Adam and included Abraham, Moses and Jesus.

Mohammed was born in about AD 570. He despised the city's corruption and the worship of many different gods that was practised there. When he was about 40 years old he received his first revelation (message from God), but when he began to preach in the city he was persecuted. He and his followers then fled to Medina, where he was well received. In 630 he returned to Mecca, but died two years later. Mohammed's revelation was later recorded in the Moslems' holy book, the Koran, which has 114 chapters and 6,263 verses. It is written in Arabic.

Islam means "submission", and Moslems believe it is a duty to submit to the will of Allah, the One True God. Religious duties and rules of behaviour are set out in the Koran and in the Hadith (the sayings and deeds of Mohammed). Behaviour that is forbidden includes gambling and eating certain "unclean" foods.

The central beliefs are called the **Five Pillars of Islam**. They are:

1 To profess the faith ("There is no god but God, and Mohammed is the Messenger of God").
2 Prayer (Arabic, *salat*). There are no priests in Islam, because every Moslem speaks directly to God.
3 Charity (Arabic, *zakat*). All things belong to God, but wealth is purified by giving to those who are in need.
4 Fasting (Arabic, *sawn*). During the month of Ramadan, Moslems fast from sunrise to sunset, without even drinking water.
5 Pilgrimage (Arabic, *haj*). All Moslems are required to make the holy journey to Mecca, if they can afford it and are well enough, once in their lives.

USEFUL ADDRESSES

● ROYAL EMBASSY OF SAUDI ARABIA
15 Curzon Street, London W1
Provides help with general enquiries
● SAUDI ARABIAN INFORMATION CENTRE
18 Cavendish Square, London W1
Provides information on living and working in Saudi Arabia.
● ISLAMIC CULTURAL CENTRE
146 Park Road, London NW8

BOOKS ABOUT SAUDI ARABIA

Passport to Arabia, Mike Gerrad, Serpents Tail 1993 (age 9–11)
Oil, Graham Rickard, Wayland 1992 (age 8–11)

GLOSSARY

ALFALFA
A crop, also known as lucerne, grown for animal feed.

COURSING
Using trained dogs to hunt and catch prey.

DESALINATION
A process that takes the salt out of seawater to make it fit to drink or to water crops.

DUGONG
A large marine mammal, also known as the sea-cow, which lives on vegetation alone.

EXPATRIATE
A foreigner who is living in another country to work.

FOSSIL WATER
Water that fell as rain centuries ago and is stored in natural reservoirs underground.

HAJ
The Moslem pilgrimage to Mecca.

HYDROPONICS
Growing plants without soil, in water enriched with chemical nutrients.

IMAM
Arabic word for a Moslem religious leader.

IRRIGATION
Artificial water supply for cultivating crops, for example using water channels and mechanized sprinklers.

KORAN
Arabic word for the holy book of Islam.

MADRASSAH
Arabic word for a Moslem school where children are instructed in Koranic knowledge.

MAJLIS
Arabic word for a meeting where the King or tribal leader hears complaints and settles disputes.

MANGROVE
A tree tolerant of salt water that grows in muddy tidal swamps in the Tropics.

MONSOON
From the Arabic word for season ("mawsim"), usually meaning seasonal rains.

MOSQUE
Moslem place of worship.

MUEZZIN
Arabic word for the man who calls the Moslem faithful to prayer at a mosque.

MUTAWA
Arabic word for the religious police in Saudi Arabia, who enforce rules of behaviour.

NOMADS
People who move from place to place with their livestock to take advantage of seasonal grazing and water supplies.

PENINSULA
Area of land with water on three sides.

PILGRIMAGE
A journey to worship at a holy shrine.

QADI
Arabic word for a religious judge at a Shariah court.

SHAMAL
A cold and dust-bearing north-east wind of Arabia.

SHARIAH
Arabic name for the Islamic system of law.

SOUK
Arabic word for a bazaar or market, often a series of covered alleys, with special areas for the sale of different goods, such as gold or spices.

TAMARISK
A salt- and drought-resistant tree, adapted to desert conditions.

TERRACES
Man-made fields that are built by levelling sections of hillsides.

WADI
Arabic word for a seasonal river bed.

INDEX

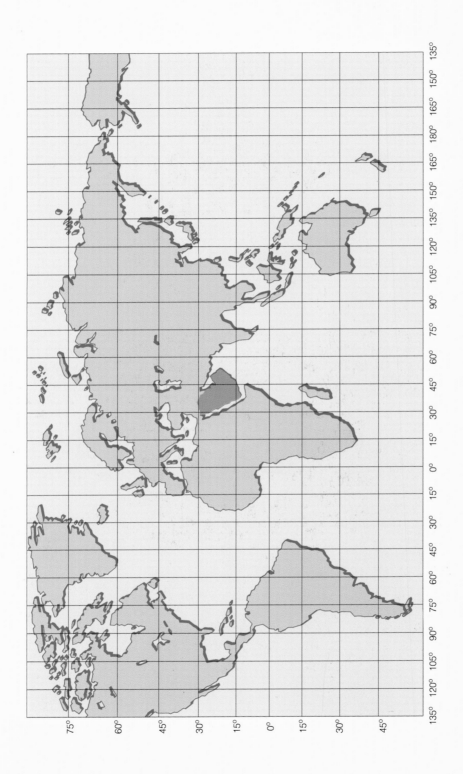